*All the Best
to
Wendy & Matt
X*

BLESSINGS

*Bernice Lever
Dec. 13, 2002.*

BLESSINGS

BERNICE LEVER

BLACK MOSS PRESS

2000

Published by Black Moss Press at 2450 Byng Road, Windsor, Ontario, Canada N8W 3E8. Black Moss books are distributed in Canada and the U.S. by Firefly Books. All orders should be directed there.

Black Moss would like to acknowledge the Canada Council for the Arts for its publishing program. Thanks also go to the Ontario Arts Council for its assistance this year.

Edited by: John B. Lee, Brantford, Ontario
Cover Art: Gordon I. Fisher, Fisher Design, Vancouver, B.C.

Cataloguing in Publication Data
Lever, Bernice
    Blessings

Poems
ISBN 0-88753-350-7

    I. Title.
PS8573.E953B64 2000   C811'.54   C00-901179-X
PR9199.3.L49B64 2000

To my children

Gordon Fisher
Janet Connolly
Melanie Lever

HEIFER DUST

My life has been
like a lover
      warm in bed
but crying at dawn
as the light
      dispels the dream.

Contents

THE BALANCED ECOLOGIST

I like things in balance,
no waste, no excess,
- one scoop of ice cream each -
saving fuel and water,
sharing beds, bathing together,

Maybe your thing is collecting
cardboard, aluminum or Saran Wrap
to be converted, recycled -
Okay, I didn't invent this world
all this disposable garbage -

But I'm willing to eat capsule
news releases printed on
vitaminized breakfast paper,
and return all my beer bottles,
jam jars, plastic packages,
and even myself for a refill
of unpolluted air and water
to wherever they're being stored.

I'd like to believe that people
could return each resource
without changing it,
   It's just ——

NOT JUST MY BUNIONS

Not just my bunions,
they're not that unique:
      red balls in summer,
      purple onions when cold,
cracking the shiny leather
of fashionable shoes,
bulging the sides of slippers,
      perhaps they miss the beat
      when I'm dancing
by their legacy of curved space.

Not just that my whole understanding
      is deformed:
my nose is crooked, too.
It heads left as I move ahead:
      of no use, the hours I spent
      pushing it right with my fist,
      my elbow braced on a wooden school desk,
it has a direction of its own.

My teeth, with early independence,
      left on their own accord,
my eyes keep clicking the dimmer switch
      refusing to focus
on my expanding, free form waistline,
my ears hear their own tune,
while my mouth sings another:
      all that enters me is changed.

All of me escapes ideal:
      not just my bulky bunions,
there are other things,
      I have my excuses -
      barriers against love.

MICA EYES

What if there were
          no more toads,
whence then
          our princes?

Skin like armour,
yet rainbow beauty
          when held close.

Their songs teach
          others to sing
as their hearts withstand
          the seasons' extremes.

Toads' eyes never blink
          at lies.

Without toads,
          princesses languish.

SHIFT ANOTHER LOAD, TOAD

Croak your sympathy, phony,
telling again
how you are that king
who builds rainbows
of greed for all.

Take, take, take,
your voice is loudest,
your belly whitest;
Oh, knobbly, wobbly, slack balls of skin,
reign disdain in your unique universe of foam.

Your pond's but a tear
from His eternal eye
shed in laughter
at your antics.

2,000 YEARS BEHIND THE TIMES

How could I ever
have called you, Toad?
That admits of
form and flesh.
and you are less
- a shifting virus -
spreading soul sickness.

Having lost Pascal's wager,
how will you explain
your abused poetic talents
to the one God
you cannot blaspheme
out of being?

You can only
          pace your page
before dark yawning death ignores
          your silly surprise
at missed bliss.

AMERICA. CALLING AMERICA

This is Broadcast One
from Radio Free Canada.
Can you hear us,
America?
We have one hour
between our winters
to thaw your heart.

We don't want to judge you
by your army deserters,
or your loud tourists,
or your company bosses,
or your ivory-towered professors,
but that's all you
send us.

Listen:
Yankee World President,
Hate kills
but hunger isn't kinder.

HAVE YOU EVER

Have you ever
thought
that the blind
have no colour prejudices,
and the deaf care
not for speeches,
etc.,

but even lacking our five
over-rated senses,
people have the choice
to hate

      or

            to love?

PRAYER

I don't want to live
everyday
as the last day,
grasping and clasping
at disintegrating care
       like a fish leaping
       from an oil slick
       into our polluted air.

Grant me the wisdom
to live each day
as the first day,
       shy in its newness
       strong in its promise.

CHILD BIRTH

Not moments
of wrenching -
        dentist tearing
        molar from
        blood gushing socket -
but hours of
strained stretching.

Not frozen, either
but searing -
        lit cigarette
        in the palm.

But huge jarrings
of the centre anchor -
        hips collapse in;
soul cuts loose

exalted in two.

ABORTION

Nurses pour living
blood into my body:
then
            answer my question,
"Oh, down in the premed. lab."

I envisage a pickling bottle
            labelled:
  (Fetus - 4 1/2 mo. - male)

Pills and drugs
and a doctor a day,
            soon I can sit
            and clean the brown
            from under my fingernails,
knowing why Lady Macbeth
is still washing her hands.

DIVORCE

A death
with no burial,
zombied in-laws lurk
at ex-anniversaries.

A scar
with no health,
has the diseased member
stayed or left?

A birth
with no promise,
un-named and un-gifted,
            a second coming.

MENTAL ADULTERY

Mental adultery
is every time
perfect.

We explained it
as sex
at first sight.

His hands came
as if I were
a tin of beans
and he had
no can opener.

Fresh from a
pain/pleasure school
and too many late night movies
of Dracula counting,
his teeth came.

Battered and bruised,
he named my body
beautiful:

Unconvinced
that violence
is no measure
of passion.

THE BEAUTY OF A WOMAN

They're really quite suited to their role,
Well, Bill, you know what I mean-
Dirt doesn't bother them,
seems to slide off their white hands;
they can go from shitty diapers
to kneading French bread in minutes.

Just built for it, I reckon;
old, moldy cheese odour of socks,
salt stiff sweaty shirts
or even stained woolen long Johns
are just everyday chores to them.

Nothing seems to upset them;
they can muck in the garden with horse manure
when planting crocus bulbs
then shape hamburger patties for dinner.

Just naturals at it, singing along with the dishes;
Marvellous really, a woman,
their soft hands can make you feel like a king.

It must be in their genes;
Just about the best thing
you can live with;
They can do everything for
a man's comfort.

Many even work, work for money,
        I mean, as well;
Able to do two things at once,
That's the beauty of a woman.

RASPED HER SKIN AWAY

First, parents scratched her eyes,
then lovers chewed
off ear lobes, ends of hair;
these can be hidden
by careful grooming & sunglasses.
A daughter stretched her belly & breasts;
these were starved back to size 8.

Now work proposals & projects wrench
off toe nails, hang nails, funny bones;
gloves & shoes can only cover so much.
Finally, a departing husband rips out
her centre.

Feeling acutely every change in the weather,
arms folded defensively, emptied
she leans in the doorway
like a skinned rabbit.

DARK PORT HOLES

(for Newlove's Black Night Windows)

Dark port holes:
sea spray splashes
the misted glass;

a listless foam
urged by waves
dying in the distance;

the sun gone down;
the moon lost
in dark clouds

as this ship
as our lives.

OoooH MACHINE

A talking machine
invited me to come
to a machine scene
that moves to music.

Restless for diversion
I enter an up and down machine
for fast action
to a road machine

which I soon leave
for a tunnel machine
at whose station I heave
coins into a food machine.

Another lot of has-been
machines return me
to a cleaning machine
for a computed rest period.

Dreaming with a friend machine
of finding a God machine
so once again I can mean
and worship what has been.

DARBY & JOAN

She got the bad weather;
> went shopping, umbrella overhead;
he got the good and a briefcase,
> went to paying job.

They never had a spit nor spat,
> never went indoors together,
changeable weather
> always kept them apart.

WEATHER A MARRIAGE

Darby & Joan; compatible mates
each with a door of their own,
they never clashed over
whose turn it was to wash up
or change the snow tires;
moving in preordained precision,
they knew who was out
         and who was in.

SOMETIMES THE DISTANCE

Sometimes the distance
between your smile
and my eyes is so great,
unable to avoid the obstacles
my heart falls into the abyss
halfway to love;

Sometimes the distance
in your eyes is so deep,
you are a continent away,
so the ocean's roar
swallows my words,
and we touch
without feeling
together;

Sometimes the distance
of overseas calls is so expensive,
each phrase is rushed,
awkward and unconnected,
yet I heard your tears
and the stone in my heart
dissolved in the pain
of your caring.

Sometimes the distance
is a challenge
worth conquering
together.

BETTER TO LOVE ROSES

Their thorns are visible, sharp and spaced,
no sly exterior to disguise danger;
Their seasons known, welcomed, a constancy
fulfilling our desire for sensuousness;
Their velvet petal's palette answers
every appetite for colour.
Finely serrated leaves play court to the blooms
whose vibrancy cheers us
by the positive thrust of their upward stems.
Their intricacy of firmly fitted layers
avoids boredom.

As the rose opens up, our hearts expand;
they are laughter in the pain of rain.
Oh, international rose,
          even Tokyo Rose,
surviving snow and sickle
from Poland to Chile,
your variety is more astonishing
than pearls from the sea.

WAKING UP

Waking up with a stranger,
the early morning light
so bright with summer
it adds a sheen to your shoes so
properly aligned with the closet door.
Even the folds of our clothes
over the soft back of the rocking chair
seem comfortable
while my neck is cramped, half off the pillow.

In such unaccustomed clarity,
the desk calendar gleams with figures:
a motel room or travel brochure photo?
Yet the uneven breathing in my ear
is just short of a snore
exhaling a mixture of musk deodorant
and last night's garlic & wine pasta.

Then the curve of a tanned shoulder
is glimpsed from the corner of my eye
as I fight the impulse to jump up:
that panicky message to leave
quickly before the other awakes.

Just last night, it seemed such a good idea,
all that excitement and heat together:
being one against the darkness,
children in awe.

But this simple sunrise shows
I don't know who you are
after twenty years of sunlight, moonlight,
stormy days without light,
so I wake up to find
you - a stranger.

BURY GUILT

Of course, it's here inside you somewhere,
but first you have to contain it —

While waiting to plan a removal method,
think on how to tell the healthy cells
from the black cancerous ones;
is there a knife sharp enough
to separate the two without blood,
without that telltale scar
that demands explanation again & again?

The trick, of course, is to sneak up on guilt,
catch it unawares, snaring it away
from all the vital organs before it
has had a chance to hook
its claws into anything important.

Once outside the body,
guilt is so innocuous looking:
a grey glue slop, a giant raw oyster,
a clearing from someone else's throat.

Surprising how much pressure it caused,
threatening to take over the whole memory bank
and   how such a small, slippery critter
took so long to identify, to trap.

But like all innocent objects,
do not touch it with your bare hands,
or some guilt is certain to cling
under your fingernails and enter you
once more when you least expect it;
in the simple act of licking your finger
to turn the page, zap —

and guilt is inside you again, ready
to spring at any of your satisfactions.

But here outside you, lying alone
on the plastic table top,
now deprived of your creative juices,
guilt begins to dry and to shrink:
        darkening a little with panic
        and with a musty, moldy smell.

So with asbestos lined, fireman's gloves
and a pair of long handled BBQ tongs
pinch guilt and plop it
into a one inch thick lead box,
immediately seal tight the lid
with copper solder from a neighbouring plumber,
bury the box under the floor boards,
steel rivet these in place
and then set your heaviest reading chair
over the hidden amputation.

Next sit down in this stuffed arm chair
which may tremble a bit as rivets pop,
so take pen and paper, to start planning
- now that your first case of guilt is contained-
how to deal with your next attack.

POOLS

That day you were
       the water, I was flesh —
floating on you, stroking
my way from end to end,
sliding, caressing, you shaping me,
       last night's wine, my buoy,
yet your words are wind-filled sails
       tugging at me,
sun sparkles lit the blue
       shadows of eyes,
azaleas perfumed the air
       but I was heady with your scent,
       fingers flowing together, compressing
       space, tense tingling,
       then circling, fanning out, withdrawing,
       shoulders curving past buttocks,
lush lapping of waves
       mapping my thighs,
then letting the sun nearly dry my skin
soon rejecting, this burning cement
       and velvet-cut towels,
my warm surface craving your touch
till separation is no longer bearable,
       I enter the water again
       you enter me, bear me
       in shared rhythms,
moist music flows between us,
       streaming over my cries,
       swimsuit discarded as nipples
       and hair rippled in your water,
my new dimensions,
       aching and arching,
supported in a wet world
where dimensions swirled

and only air breaks mattered,
          our circuit is one,
keep turning me,
          fluidity: a way of life
with the taste of petals in my mouth,
          you were flesh —
                    I was water.

I WANT A STUD FOR A WEEK

I WANT
some bucking stallion
who has been prancing around
his isolated paddock
with only a whiff
with each hourly breeze
of the neighing mares
from fields far away
to whet his appetite — so
give us green pastures
to romp in.

I WANT
a stud so in heat
that his semen is white hot —
searing enough to match my desire;
no gentle, perfumed caresses, please.

I WANT
to be mounted and rammed
past the oozing moisture stage
to the tearing of burning dry tissue —
let the lips of my vagina
rasp off skin until blood
is our only lubricant,
rearing and thrusting
past climax after next summit,
past need, and beyond
to the burn-out of emotion and flesh,
hormones to ash,
all nerve-endings dead —

I WANT
to be finally spent
then let wounds heal,
seal together the jagged edges
forming into one black,
impenetrable scar mass —

I WANT
to be done with sex,
to be free
          to get on.

HARMLESS FUN

What harm could there be
in undressing for dinner,
just prance around his kitchen
in my lace garter belt,
sheer nylons, high heels?

All I had to do, he said,
was to serve with a smile and
avoid the spitting cooking oil
and, I thought, pretend
I don't look ludicrous
or begging an appointment
with my chiropractor.

Why thirty years ago
spike heels were easier
to balance on,
and now it seems
I lose my upright position
every time
I try to straighten the seams
in these glamour stockings.

Also waxed kitchen tiles
don't cushion my fall
from grace.

Why worry if my middle age middle
seems to bulge larger
than my freckled breasts
leering from their satin
pushup cups?

ON HAVING LOVERS

"On" being the crucial word
'cause mostly it's "off",
being put off, rained-out, postponed,
when spouse or previous lover or only mother
enters the warming-up pit,
up-staged, out-positioned, delayed,
until they can fit you in,
into their dug-out,
never a "home" game, always playing
at the visiting town.

Does one have an "in" with a lover
or even a favourable "inning",
yet never a home run,
no matter how many times
you knock the ball out of the park.

Lovers are contagious, an addictive sport;
one leads to another, a strike-out;
a new lover helps you
over the last one: a no-hitter;
there seems no cure:
            only withdrawal symptoms,
no preventives:
            only The Pill, just more
of the same bad medicine
repeating in your stomach
            and a cold hollowness
with "good-bye" on your lips,
when your batting average is down
when you can't quite cheer
or wish your lover "farewell"
as you're always sliding
towards base, never quite touching.

So who's the umpire
and who's keeping score
or even the players straight
and waving pennants for the winning side?
        But players run for the highest pay,
not for team loyalty.
Even the playing field has fake turf today.

BEING TOTALLED

"I told you before, bitch,"
his words shouted over the crashing of my novel
across the room, pages flapping
"not to read when I'm around."

I hadn't heard his car parking,
his rubber fishing boots mounting
the front wooden steps
or his opening the door, rod in hand,
as I read Jane Austen's polite talk
         — lost in books where
            husbands never beat their wives —

He grabs my shoulders in a pliers-grip
just as sudden as his entrance
snapping me to my feet;
with adrenalin racing, I duck my head,
trying to avoid the inevitable
back-handed smack across the face;
cornered in front of the red canvas chair
I think, at least, another nose bleed won't show;
silently, I try to dodge the blows
which always begin slowly,
lined up with eyes sharp with hate
while I attempt to focus on
         where the children are;
can they hear us   — can they see us?
Pray, God, they're sound asleep.

I force my energies into escape, just
getting free of his hold on my right biceps
but his fingers on my right arm bite deeper
as his free fist aims at a new spot.
         No use to scream as that only angers him more

and as the town lawyer said,"You need 2 witnesses who are not
      relatives. Otherwise, self-defence, you know,
        he will claim you attacked him."
and the town cop said, "No, lady, I can't come up, 'cause
      I'm on duty alone and
        somethin' important might happen."

So who is there to save me from this nightmare?
As hurt hammers away any comforting images
of witty drawing room conversation or
Hallmark cards of brides in long, lacy gowns,
I brace my knee against his hip
trying to break free,   but
careful not to inflict any pain in return
as that only increases his violence, his temper.

And why is he angry this time?
Did I forget to water the new tomato plants,
or did his girl friend not turn up
for the weekend fishing trip?   She or I,
what does it matter? The effect is the same;
he wants me to suffer for his loss,
for whatever he senses that I, others, enjoy,
whatever it is that he cannot embrace.
Helplessness fuels his rage
as he gets more intent on landing a few decent
punches, ones that mark,
ones that tell me he is boss here.

As the pain becomes more than I can stand,
I let myself go limp as my dinner rises in my throat
so my knees sag, yet I remain
conscious as I slip to the floor;
his hands grab at my already choking neck,
and I hope he will choke me this time.
I no longer want to yell, stop, as I know

if he stops, all this will happen
        bruises, swollen eyes, cracked ribs
all happen again,
so I pray for death, this time, now;
I want this all to be finished,
so I call out,
        "Hit me, hit me, more, again."

Lying there spread-eagled as always,
he on knees and elbows,
now he has what he wanted: submission;
now he is aroused: desperate to join me;
I'm gasping for air, licking blood from a split lip,
as he tears down my panties;
his hands sliding up under my dress,
he grasps my breasts for anchors
as he enters me, lunging and banging
against my pubic bone,
trying to smash his way to my centre;
me hating myself for taking any pleasure
from his thrusting violence, but
eventually he collapses, spent.

His arms cradling me, his beery breath
whispers softly in my swollen ear,
        "Sorry, I need you; I love you;
        I don't want to hurt you anymore.
        Please love me."
All those words I've been longing to hear
and wanted presented
        with bouquets and perfume
now come tumbling out sleepily
as bruises blossom in my flesh.

A CRYING SHAME

(for a million women)

All those silly white lies
that no one believes,
but with common conspiracy,
they nod in agreement:
>"Just wearin' a scarf
>'cause I forgot to curl my hair."
>or "Always wear long sleeves
>'cause I burn so easy-like."

for Arlene keeps hiding.

They all know at that local corner store
that what Arlene's covering up
is what he did to her
after another night of bad hands, worse bets
and too much drink from
the thought of losing the grocery money
again at the Saturday poker game.

It's Monday morning, and Arlene's asking
for credit again,
>"'cause Joe forgot to give
>me the grocery money agin."

The next door neighbours probably heard her cries,
but it's not right to interfere
between a man and his wife,

So on this hot July morning, in the clean mountain air,
Arlene's trying to get some bread and milk,
maybe even a little sliced bologna for her kids
as she flushes redder from an inner heat
while pretending she's not battered

"black 'n blue", knowing that by next Friday
when the soreness is gone,
the marks will have grown larger
but fainter, as purple and brown centres
fade to a sick yellow and green
as Arlene continues to overdress
for summer,
afraid to admit the evidence
to herself,
yet sensing, as she leaves the store
where the cashier's eyes are full of pity,
the clucking tongues along the grocery aisles
chirp, "What a cryin' shame."

MAN OVERBOARD

Here I am left alone
in the boat
with your empty space
trying to steer a course
with only one paddle.

Leaning from side to side
dipping my paddle deep
into the foaming water
I circle crazily
splashing uselessly
unable to see where
you disappeared from our vessel.

It finds the shore only
when we both paddle together.

DIVORCE IS LIKE A HOCKEY GAME

Divorce proceeds like a hockey game,
but seldom is there time out
        just lots of body checks
a rush of wingers
        about to be benched
for high sticking is common
as is scoring from the end zone,

Certainly, no rest between periods
and no boarding now
        just choosing up sides
measuring each other's defensive play
which is always over the blue line
and more than the puck is off side.
These legal referees take your money   and
give no penalties for bloodying your opponent;
here I am not disbarred from the game
for permanent damage to the other.

Divorce is a modern spectator sport
with more subtle carnage
than feeding Christians to the lions;
now non-believers and believers alike
are shredded by LOVE: that 4 letter word.

Old timers line the front rows,
even lean over the boards towards the ice,
shouting encouragement !
about how they would score
if they had the chance to shoot again.
I feel the need of dressing rooms,
hot showers and bandage wraps,
plastic shin guards and a metal face mask
before facing the judge, knowing

I can't score the winning goal,
that this game carries no bonus points
because we missed the couple's playoffs:
no international championship cup for us.

SPARE GOD BOREDOM

God created the world in seven days
having a natural feeling for the week
or just being a seven limbed creature.

In fact, the seventh day was one of rest
which was when the Garden of Eden
seemed a good idea — a State of the Art creation —
a first vision of paradise,
a pastel garden with no winter.

Also Adam was Her dream of a balanced, 4 limbed being;
Eve grew from God's understanding of loneliness,
and someone had to wash the dishes
but the attraction of perfection is short-lived.

So God took on the eternal challenge:
she and her mirror buddy,
the one who always told her that she was the fairest one,
that horned ham, that guy in the red satin cloak,
              would vie for our attention.

So each new boy and girl baby
were given unique weaknesses and talents,
so we keep having our random
little triumphs and tiny tragedies,
pratfalls and trophies;

Adam and Eve, those first models,
were given an insatiable hunger for knowledge
and began the human quest toward infinity

so we are still falling;

the rest is history:

we spare God her boredom.

THE STRANGEST FACE

("...the strangest glimpses you may have of any creature in the distant
lands will be those you catch of yourself."
Margaret Laurence: *The Prophet's Camel Bell*)

Is there no still pond, Narcissus,
to give me back my illusions of myself,
no whole person?
Just these shallow changeable surfaces:

1. — the cracked bar room mirror
reflects my eyebrows at three levels,
my lipstick trio of mouths garish
in neon light mumble triple lies
while I ask myself, "What am I doing here?"
with someone else's lover
at this beer stained table
in this noisy, nicotine fog —

2. — or thin lipped anger compressed
on metal table tops as
salespeople chat about their holidays
as I await service, even notice
that I am not a dumb mannequin —

3. — or the operating room mirrors
so bevelled that they balloon
my plump, grinning features
from beaming madonna
to birthing madwoman—

4. — and my cheeks askew
double din your moist eyes
that say, "She's gone, too late."
and I am left with
this pale pair of ovals of my face floating
unsteadily in your sorrow.

EMILY CARR, CENTRIFUGAL ARTIST

Emily, you who taught whole
       landscapes to dance,
       your brush strokes escaping the canvas edge,
       taking each viewer to circling vistas
       cresting with each new wave of energy,
became essence diviner.

Emily, you who carved in colour
       and put silence in motion,
       then whirled your forests
       about breathlessly,
were spirit painter.

Emily, you who gave us our land
       codified to a new grandeur
       teasing our primitive imaginations,
       awakening a hunger in each viewer
by setting a horizon that none have surpassed
and claimed your own borders of magnificence.

THE NEW WOMAN

she learns — the tricks of the trade and trades in her old suburban image for The New Woman,

she wears — brand labels: Hugh Hefner bras, Gucci leathers, and the latest little purple plastic pins with matching cheekbones and fingernails.

she smells — sanitized, sterilized, floralized and expensive,

she reads — Greer for career, Flare for fashion and Margaret Mead for history,

she works — full time, all the time, on anyone's time and place,

she plays — at squash, at work and competes at play for playthings,

she eats — alfalfa sprouts, sugar-free yogurt and whole grain pumpkin bread,

she drinks — pretty cocktails, but 1929 wine, if you're buying,

she takes — vitamins, minerals and gifts of stocks & bonds,

she drives — whatever man steers the silver Porsche and leases the penthouse with the 4 bathrooms,

she sleeps — around anyone's little finger,

she loves — when it's not too much commitment; it suits her career, and it pleases her analyst,

she believes — in others, if they believe in her.

50

BEING HATED

When I am first hated :
        the scab is rough, irregular,
        lumpy even, crisp at the edges;
        I lift one rim a little,
        bleeding relieves the pressure
        for awhile.
        While it never heals,
        there are days when I
        do not notice it.

What antidote for hate:
        this diseased connection,
        history present as a scab,
its angry red: colouring our words,
its yellow pus: fouling our sight.

How did this festering scar tissue
        grow between us:
slowly like a bruise
        of an undone favour,
quickly like a scratch
        of an unkind retort,
or the cut of laughter
        not shared?

AS IF CARBON IS NOTHING

At the crematorium for my first visit,
I snap the seat belt around you
for the last time,
wondering what it is that I am
securing on the passenger seat.

This is all that remains:
a box not big enough for snow boots,
a heavy rectangle of cardboard
and anonymous brown paper,
with an official receipt and certificate
stating the name of the deceased,
trying to prove that something of value
is contained by scotch-taped corners
that the family now has
its money's worth.

Grandfather lives a little life
with a chip on his lip,
then crumbles into dust
or chars into ash,
though no one will lift
a shovel to dig
that final hole,
the so-called resting place,
as if these burnt specks
could someday be awakened.

What a ritual farce
we play,
trying to bury our own fears.

UNABLE TO SWAY YOU, FATHER

Pounding my fists
on your fat chest,
the hollow rhythmic thump
of my anger erupting from the empty
surprise of your mouth,

you, not even rocking
back on your work boot heels,
your very body a fortress
mocking my outburst

my sixteen year old anger
just a fourth daughter's frustrations
      neither my flailing poems
      nor drumming knuckles
made any sense to you
who could not know my outrage

with these siblings
narrow as the wooden slats
that half-blocked the hot air vents,
in that mountain house
you so carefully built,
a home we so recklessly split,
easily as kindling.

SUE HENRY & I DOIN' TIME

And which of us is more caged?
I with my clever creative writing exercises
all mentally rehearsed to program you,
a talented Canadian Indian poet,
doin' time on the inside   and
me mainly filling time on the outside.
          Big sloppy Sue, a brown girl wearing
runners, not moccasins, and writing
gentle love lyrics with pudgy fingers;
your shirt tails hanging out over the bulge
above your wide-leather belted jeans,
your approach direct; "Well, lady, what's in it for you?"
     "No, I'm not getting paid, just volunteering my time,
     giving my time away" —so — so I could feel superior or
     maybe more privileged than you   who are paying
     this country for your crimes in time:
     2 years less a day of your time.
"Well, lady, you think we got time on our hands in here?"
     "Yes, all your meals, everything provided; there must be lots of free
     time."
     "Well, lady, we gets kitchen duty, laundry duty, an' spendin' time
with our pasty pastor, our clink shrink, patsy parole officer, an' everyone
hassling you to take time for some classes:
hairdressing, typing an' with some study time,so you can support yourself
after — yeah, my holiday on the inside. Passin' this time, ain't like passin'
a joint, you know that, lady?"
Her accepting grin softened her words.
     "Isn't there any free time?"
"Inside here, lady? It's paid time, heavy times, real hard time in solitary."
Sue's brown eyes were no longer joking.
     "But solitary was outlawed, proclaimed in parliament as unjust,
cruel treatment, and all that!"
"Well, lady, just try sharing time in here, a little fun time, maybe
hug your girl in the shower! Hell, you'll be slammed into isolation

faster than you can say, 'Now, class, time for metaphors.'
It's all you do-gooders out there in the middle-class;
you have time on your hands. Our hands is empty."

Now I have time to remember:
Sue Henry, single parent of two,
lover of guys and gals,
took ~~ptomaine~~ her teeth   *time*
and floated free of our space
in one final bust-out.

PEACE

It's all of a piece, as my aunt Kay would have said:
everything is connected,
but not seamless and with lots of patching,
yet no separate yours and mine,
just one earth
that shares each bit of pollution
as evenly as the dust from Krakatau
donated glowing sunsets
for two years world-wide,
beauty and warning free
to both the rich and the poor.

Oceans of land and water
circle this globe
in mapped and known shapes,
soon to be obliterated.

As I breathe in air which contains
in just one lungful, some atoms
from the bodies of Jesus Christ
and a crusty dinosaur,
my blood circulates oxygen
that recently was exhaled
by Chinese rice farmers   and
diapered babies in Brazil.

Scientists can compute how many times
this glass of water has been drunk before
and what queens will swallow it next,
and estimate howl long we will have water to drink
once we atom bomb this one earth
to a dry cinder.
            That's all or peace.

WAITING

Some say waiting is the worst:
just what is beyond the sunset
so worry stops our steps
into that dark,

but when wrong ruts get entered
how many would wish for uncertainty
rather than this certain misery?

But change for good or worse
is short-changed
when we jam up
just waiting for the verdict
and afraid it is the one sentence
we cannot make our lips mouth.

Our fear freeze-frames
into black and white stereotypes
of winners and losers,
but it seems our side is always
slipping down the red debit avalanche,

unable to prepare rescue units
for which alternative
is about to overtake
our waiting.

ADVICE

And what have I to give?
Just a list of my failures:
>   slammed in my face doors
>   or snickering rejections
>   or plain icicle silences
freezing my bravado retorts
of "I don't care!"
when the whole block knows
I'm desperate for acceptance
>   just a hug to affirm
>   I am worth touching
but so often shunned as the leper
as others keep their gloves on
but still their claws cut
from across the crowded room.

How could I advise anyone about anything?
Me — just a non-model —
so why try to second guess the fates
or ever question the heart;
how can logic win
against this chaos called life?
Percentages are no guarantee;
what worked for a thousand others
will surely fail for me,
or if I suggest a path for you,
the black trap will spring shut.

DISPLAY

A bad hair day
is unimportant,
so forget your pimply skin
'cause surfaces never last.

Exercise your spirit
until it's shining
with good will,
not with "Have a good day!"
with a fake smile
set in place with spray,
mousse or gels.

But don't worry
about exterior details,
'cause a loving, pumping
red heart lasts
longer than brand name
sweat shirts
that nobody sweats in anymore
or the latest running shoes
for bar stool display.

So heal inner blemishes of blame
and festering sores of sourness.

Let others see the inside of you:
show your unique fun and fire
as fashions flare and fade,
~~but~~ 'cause you'll last 100 years
if you cherish you.

THEY

They smiled
when they splashed me
in mud puddles;

They grinned
when they dumped me
in garbage bins;

They laughed loudly
when they dropped me
head first   down
that outhouse hole,

Then I was small
     and they were big,

Then I was weak
     and they were wrong,

But only strong in muscle and bone.

My spirit was never alone:
     others washed me in tears
     clean hands held mine
and the Lord answered my painful prayers.

Now I am healing,
     my scars are fading
          and I pity them
as the child is remembered with love
by the adult self: a hand in a well-worn glove.

IT'S SO HARD TO HURT THE DEAD!

for Janet and Melanie

If only I had known earlier,
            when he was alive,
            then I could have taken revenge,
but no use now
            if child confesses this...

How to stop my mind's eye fixation
on this too late revealed scene:
            the slim four year old
            in the upstairs bathroom,
            she can't reach that high door hook, and
the coaxing voice of the burly grandfather,
    "Look at it, Girlie, it's too big for you now,
    Look at what it does, someday...."

or the budding eleven year old:
            she's not tall enough to get her nose
            above his pinning shoulder,
struggling to breathe
beneath the 212 pounds of granddad
urging her to relax and enjoy,
            "It won't hurt, girlie, just let it touch you,
    Put it between your legs, someday..."

This unlabelled enemy is safe:
            his wrongs cannot be righted
            nor injustices balanced.

Would it help to unbury the casket,
            have a ceremonial fire,
            then dump the ashes in the sewer
            where they belong,

melt the brass grave marker into a bed pan,
       erase the name from the family tree
or write a true history?

Do something now —spit on the lie,
       create a new memory.
Enough! nor more generations
       to suffer the sickness.

INCONVENIENT

Now there is no place
to put Mother,
not a free corner
in which to stash old Mom.

I am inconvenient
arriving in the midst of your summer
schedule already full of fun
and other young people.

You say, perhaps in one or two years,
you'll have a guest room.

I am a non-guest!
          How has someone so familiar
          become an inconvenient stranger?

Now thirty-eight years later,
          I feel the wrenching
          pain of a miscarriage
draining me.

Have I lived too long?
          Yet the time between injury
          and healing is faster now
          accelerating to nil.

Sorry, time for Mother
          to grow up,
leave her children
as if three thousand miles
          of earth's crust
          were not enough;
my last cherished myth is dust.

EYE WELLS

eyes narrowed as holes,
end openings of a double-
barrelled shot gun

seem to transfix me
as you squint astride sun-
dried, beached logs.

Do I narrow your field of vision
or do you want to see only
    a little of me at a time
or am I too much to stomach whole
or are you afraid I'll see
    too deeply inside you?

Perhaps, you have nothing
            to hide, to share.

Open eyes can invite
            another, a lover in
            as a caressing invitation,
but yours are twin microscopes
studying me, making me
a dead example of something
    or other,
a specimen under glass.

BED MEMORY RIDDEN

Choking to death
on penis,
wondering who will pry
my lover loose
once rigor mortis
sets my lips

suffocating
on anus odour,
recalling wash day blues
of scrubbing
stained underwear
by hand

"This is the ultimate
pleasure
you can do for me.
Now I know
you love me."

The only buttocks
I cherish
are one year new,
      freshly dusted
      to give my lips
      a chalky coating
      of Johnson's baby powder.

WOMEN UNDERSTAND PANDAS

- the need for tender bamboo shoots

- in a red meat-crazed world

- the splayed, soft bear rug for walking on

- the sad, yellow eyes of caged bears

- the smelly, cement barred boxes in zoos

- the warm, cuddly status symbol

- the international shipping of bear bodies

- for profitable mating

- the unique collecting of prized possessions

- the insistent male urge to continue their line

   even with dominance,

      they are not complete.

DISCARD

Oh, carve me a condom of stone
  an everlasting barrier between us;
  let no one get really close to me.

Use diamond - a crystal so clear
  to see all, to cut all
  in its sharpness - cutting away
my insides until I am cleansed of desire,
  especially of desiring you.

Oh, carve me a symbolic condom
  slackly spilling seeds of every colour
  on dry flesh - seared by light
  from the ever unloving sun,
  deprived of dark, fertile places
  where moisture nurtures life.

Oh, carve me a condom of fear
  that protects hope against disease,
  avoiding possible plagues
  as sick as ecstatic states;
  just create whatever is necessary
  to keep lovers from being one.

Oh, carve me something: facile, ugly and evil
  —show me the handiwork of the devil—
  dividing people, trusting none,
  as I become a used condom.

TITLE FIGHT

We circle each other tentatively
like two old sparring partners
familiar with the size of the ring
and how soon the time goes,
so we struggle to make
each round count for something.

We try for tight, close clinches
but ones that do not mark nor mar
wanting only warm memories of our touching
as we've both had a surfeit of scars
from broken rules or common laws,
looking not for titles, but for tenderness.

I DON'T WANT THIS POWER

Take your life back,
        paste it on your own hand;
my palms are raw from fingernails digging
        into worried flesh
        that cannot relax
from this struggle to keep you
trying, trying, living.

Take your desire for life,
        pour it back into your own eyes;
my lids are raspily dry and red hot
        from refusing easy tears
        that want to replace
all my most reassuring smiles
from his effort to keep you
desiring, desiring, living.

Take your power from your pulse,
        push blood back through your heart;
my chest is aching
        from expanding for us both,
        air into exhausted lungs
wanting to rest, just one,
        from this fight to keep you
        breathing, breathing, living.

LONELY AND SMILING

The ache within
is not a pain
that pills can hide
nor doctors slice off;
no incision is deep
enough to remove
these embedded tendrils
so rooted in nerve and bone.

Only your embrace
can fill my hollow heart,
block the shadows
from blurring my smile
to sadness.

Somehow the longing
in my unmarked loneliness
is like a sliver of silver moon
on a winter's evening,
only a fraction
of that warm harvest fullness,
that meeting of season and person.

PERFECTED WITH TIME

Memories
are better than a holiday:
every holiday, whether an afternoon
            or two week stretch,
is a gamble.

You can't control the weather
or which idiot will sit next
to you on the bus or plane
or even behind you at the movies.

You never know which thief
will take what
or which virus or germ
will decide to invade your body.

At times, even if you avoid
the strikers' picked line
and closed for reno' places,
interruptions and hazards
seem more common than calm,
and your wallet always seems
empty before the vacation ends.

But you can choose a favourite memory:
the time everything went right
when you landed a big one
when you won that race
when the Other was perfect
when a warm, rusty sunset melted
after tender steaks, crisp salad
and even chilled champagne,
then warm shoreline water was just
right for walking in hand in hand

or that dance floor pulsed
in time with your matched steps,
and more pleasure not recorded here.

You can recall each caress
        remember that kiss
        relive the bliss
        perfect every time;
memories perfected with time.

EATING

With my fistful of cents-off coupons,
I enter the automatic doors
in anticipation;
today I'll find a satisfying bargain,
        a perfect fit;
gluttony feeds my imagination,
while the offered 'deals of the week'
        starve my body.
"Save! save! save!" But what is safe?

Eat, eating, ate, have been eaten:
pleasure all over now
as I am attracted
by every forbidden fruit of the 90's.
Supermarket shelves seem to be showing
row after row of enticing foods:
        tempting Italian sausages - too high in cholesterol,
        lush Hawaiian pineapple with too much fibre,
        delicious dark chocolate torte hiding its sugar,
        Mexican salsa chip dip - too spicy for my ulcers,
        crusty long sticks of French bread
suggesting the starch was baked out of them,
        crisp cucumber and salad pals
pretending they grew without pesticides,
        and all those amazing claims of low-cal
supermarket alcohol don't raise my spirits.

I keep busy, pushing my empty basket,
        searching for suitable food;
I can count calories,
but I can't remove the additives.
Yet I have my feasting memories
        when everything was chosen for delight,
        when taste was all that counted,
memories of your tongue and lips,
your hands and other things
eating.

WE BREATHE ONLY OXYGEN

Trees are dying; to the north, acid rain is eating them.
        They can't inhale much of our exhaust.
Every year more people are breathing more O_2;
        every year more babies are exhaling CO_2.
Trees being cut, de-limbed, de-barked,
        even drowned in hydro projects,
        even their roots are ploughed up and out.
Every year, fewer of them producing O_2.
        They need more than our good breath - CO_2;
        they need clean rain and fertile earth.
we keep breathing, and creating more babies;
        we only breathe by the gift of their breath.
Every minute: a giant cedar crashes down
        on the soggy west coast,
        rusty bark as thick as your wrist
        but no longer alive as your lungs.
Every minute - falling - faster, ever faster:
        a moss covered cypress, a flowering magnolia
        a pitch sticky pine, a lush bread fruit tree.
Every minute - here - there - birds flap off
        as ground squirrels scurry - where?
        as fish gasp in ash laden waters
        while wild flowers fry
        from the heat of burning stumps.
Countries of lifeless grey and black skeleton trees.
Every year more trees are disappearing;
        fewer are exhaling oxygen;
                more of us—
                      fewer of them-
yet we only breath by the gift of their breath.
Trees are dying;
        our turn is coming.

TOMORROW I WILL STEAL A BLACKJACK

I will wear my red nylon ski mitts
- you never leave your fingerprints
on the murder weapon.
I have a list of possible candidates:
am just devising criteria
or priorities for which of you
 should be first, after all,
being my first victim
should be an honour in itself.
Who wants a no-name killer,
just a run-of-the-mill mugger
who eliminated you
for being at the right place
at the wrong time?

Death by a celebrity's hand
is so much better;
high profile trials
will allow the media to highlight
every aspect and ash of your existence;
your passing will be dramatized
for TV and serialized for radio;
if talk show hosts should mouth you
to death, an original cause
makes your body a cause celebre-
black jacked!

Being struck dumb by a pack of cards,
being left to freeze naked
in a snow field in an Ontario January blizzard,
just these sets of cards adding to twenty-one
stuck under limbs - here and there-
Just jack of all trades

being hijacked out of life,
not even a proper metal,
that black steel blackjack
to pound your brains into submission-
Now no car jack will lift you into breathing;
you're just a stiff cream form
in a farmer's white field,
waiting for your 15 seconds of fame
on the local evening news, until blackout
unable to make the major leagues
of a 15 minute magazine piece on national TV -
but I will, as all my past lovers
ignore my red ski mitts
and identify my nude body walking into town,
looking for that microphone
and the cameras, to tell my story.

A TARGET

It's happened;
anyone can tell you, there is a plot:
just listen to the gossip, snide asides, innuendoes,
a smear campaign is smudging my name.
I'm disappearing,
soon no one will admit
to ever have known me.

My enemies have a plan:
writs, liens, lawsuits attack
my dwindling dollar deals,
properties flooded, and buildings burned
until my assets are in ashes.

I'm the target;
these plotters have marked me:
a bull's eye painted on my shoulder blades,
an apple balances on my head,
my shoes are filled with plastic explosive
            ready for the first time I stamp in anger;
trip wires are set for the next time
            I open that marked door,
so nitro will splash on my face
            or shiny guillotine will slice my neck.

I am replaceable. I am expendable.
  Start playing target practice
  as the line forms to the right.

HEART-TO-HEART TALKING

Please, little pump keep pumping
fat-laden, rusting blood
through this aging body;

these cooling hands and feet
need your fresh heaters:
those oxygen fuel cells;

kidneys and liver struggle
waiting for you, dear heart
to suck away their wastes
to replenish their food shelves;

stomach full, even distended
begs your engine's flow to power
its digestion and digressions;

fainting senses and sensibilities
plead for the smelling salts
of your life-line liquor
as you feed energy to my climaxes.

Your beats: the most precious music,
Oh heart, know you are loved.

HEART TALKS BACK

Endless demands
with sillier cheer leading chants:
>   go man go
fight woman fight

Well, give me a break!
>   You need this area sent
white cells for repair
>   but others sent as infection
fighters somewhere else.

Here and there, you know,
the opposite ends of this
misused mangle of muscle and bone
you call your body;
it's easy for you
you just give commands, orders,
I'm the one that has to do the work!

Next, it's your arms and legs
demanding bright red oxygen,
rich energy supplies
for those trendy aerobic classes
while your smoke and smog clogged lungs
play work-to-rule games.

Well, I've got tougher muscles
than you'll ever see on those sweaty limbs
as you punish me in the sauna
or worse, in shell-shock Polar Bear swims.

Don't ask me to calm your self -induced stress;
how many hours of sleep do I get?
Never even a forty wink cat nap

and holidays, forget them!
They're just another endurance test, for me
as you quick dry brains with margaritas,
sun sear your surface
and then expect me to help you
 impress some special sexy
senor or senorita!

    You can save your whining praises,
too late for words; no sweet syllables can repair
the damage of your temper tantrums punching me,
especially not after all the junk food
you expect me to survive on!
    My valves snap in anger
at the way you abuse me;
there ought'a be a law against....

HURTING YOU

Hurting you was never
part of my plan;
I never meant,
            "You're always a loser."
What I said was,
            "This proves you don't have a brain.
            I mean not checking the gas level!"
This doesn't mean that
I was trying to hurt you;
it was just something I had to do,
blurt out words for my own relief.

I never meant to hurt you,
but saying "sorry" never helps,
            is no excuse nor solution.
Sorry is a useless band-aid
always slipping off and
never helping to heal hurt.

What I said wasn't intended
            to hurt you;
it wasn't direct at
            you personally,
just things can go wrong at cottages.
Just a passing observation
that I did mean,
            "Remember, I was the one in labour
            in a boat out of gas!"
well, but not to be painful.

I never meant to hurt you
at first but now
I do, I do!

BEWARE PASSION, MY FRIEND

Your words pour passion
burning listening ears
until minds warm and whimper,
hearts flare and flame.

You become their life source
as they flock to your feet
to catch that lava
- searing against injustices -
from your impudent lips.

You scorch their enemies
while burying their fears
in fire, ash and pumice;
your words hot-wire their wholeness.

With gasping lungs and heated bodies,
they swarm you, wanting
just to feel your fiery surface,
as if one touch could alight them,
as if creativity is contagious.

As circling arms and legs
of those adoring trip your dancing steps,
        you hot footing it over boiling waters
until you join the choicest openings offered
- the finest matched ember
        or even promised moment's coolness -
only to discover fans are vampires
        and lips once melted together are silent.

Spent in flesh, the performer lies
        wordless.

HOW YA BEN?

- for Carol Malyon

"Lousy, can't get out of this soap opera
I'm in - just splashing around in tear
jerking suds called the bath of life."

Let's swap stories; our fantasies
must be better than our lives,
or we wouldn't be forced to create
such fictions, giving ourselves
an element of control,
shaping beginnings and endings;
we'll pretend a shape that is
not found in the endless
splotches of our lives—

Let's just hug, accept & praise
each other; why try to interpret
a dozen - or even a six pack-
of annual family disasters
that seem pale parlour jokes
now that they are over,
no longer looming as life threatening.

"How ya ben? Lousy: felt
lost and unloved coast to coast
or seemed adored from Halifax to Victoria,
depends on my season, which day you ask!"

frost flowers etch

perfect petals on tiny windows:

abandoned toy car

*   *   *

straight-backed

prairie dog guards

tire-flattened lover

*   *   *

on sunlit window sill

curled white kitten purrs

warmth in winter air

BEFORE WE WERE BORN

Oh, how   we knew
>   rough pounding of dad's belly
>   against our wet home
>   as we nestled
>   in mom's womb

Oh, how   we knew
>   sounds of curses and sighs
>   yet felt warmth of unseen sun
>   healing caresses of mom's fingers

We knew before pressuring tunnel
>   before first air suck
>   before cord-cutting final separation

Oh, how   we knew
>   love's yin and yang.

ANGELS

Angels   on my shoulder
Angels   dancing 'round my head   CHORUS
Angels   guiding my feet
Angels   guarding my heart

There are never enough   angels
Everyone needs more than one
Angels   protecting all of us
         from our own follies
Angels   with so much to be done
So we must be   angels
         to one another
travelling together

Angels   have had angel training
         Can you reach out
         But never ever shout?
Just softly, take a worn hand
Smile into the other's faded eyes
         Wordlessly,   angel-like
telling them, "You are loved."

Lessons from Angel School
         can be so cool
         but not for a fool

Have you ever had the Angel's touch?
         How to stop a heart's racing panic
         How to comfort a wailing grouch
Angel   hands,   angel   lips

Just be an angel to one another
We can reach Heaven together   (Bridge)

Angel wings waft away each leech
Angel feathers mute angry speech
Angel scares away the dark
Angel voices, sweet, soothing lark

PIECES

Just   scattered pieces
drifting on the tides
     trying to find my own way
     a few years with this partner
     or a few hours with another lover
trying to swim   against the current,
yet all around me   dirty debris,
empty wine bottles,   used condoms.

Once our moms and dads sang
     of the "rocky shores" of selfish goals;
they knew too well the difficulty of steady steps
     in the "shifting sands" of city streets.

But now everything and everyone is polluted:
     bubbling streams and blue oceans are poisoned
     with the same chemicals that foul
     our brown farmlands and hazy air.

Too many people stumble about in diseased bodies
with cancers caused by our own industries:
     the acid rain that kills our green trees
     and silver finned fish is eating us, too,
as new plagues ravish our bodies.

Yet greater still is the damage done to our minds:
     the blight of false ideas and ideals,
     the lies seeded as progressive thoughts,
     the constant contamination by the media
selling us more possessions for damnation.

We struggle in barbaric times:
  now computers suck last pennies from pensioners,
  jet screams deafen the baby's ears,
  city lights blot out the stars and
no one hears the nightingale singing.

TOMBSTONES

Advertising for the dead:
who's buying
and who's selling
reputations by the phrase?

More scanned
than LIFE magazine,
most leave wilted
forget-me-nots;
few take the stone
verses home.

Who's listening
and who's telling
that James T. Jones
one hundred years ago
was good at it?

KLEPTO

Who me? Well, maybe sometimes
I just clip a few things
little things, usually
just one at a time, you know,
pocket-sizers or less
whatever is palm size.

 I'm not a magician
no Copperfield, nor Houdini
Now you really have to admire
those guys who can disappear
 - right on stage, before your eyes -
an elephant. Wow!

"Seeing is believing" so it goes, but
no one believes this curly-haired
granny takes things,
another's things, I mean
so others never see me.

Really this matching pair
of purple linen napkins
- for your new apartment -
were just a lark
please, laugh now,
no harm done, that restaurant
got lots of 'em,
'cause for you I'd steal
the world,   well,
whatever bits would fit
in my handbag!
Really, sometimes, it's too easy
to even be fun, anymore.
Please, don't use that "maniac" word!

I'm not a keepo-maniac.
Why sometimes I don't even keep
the bright baubles,
the tip money on cafe' tables
'cause now I find
 more challenge in
returning them without
anyone noticing me.

Double duty, twice the pleasure.
How did I become invisible?

MENTAL MURDER

Murder's not funny,
at least, the victim never gets
the joke, just the punch line.
          Aren't puns killers?
Often the victim's family is not laughing,
even close friends are not smiling,
perhaps a nervous hiccup or giggle
at awkward lines in the eulogy.

But - as long as the murderer
remains outside barred cells -
she or he can enjoy success,
having committed the ultimate
that final stage of robbery,
taking another's life - not just for a holiday-
but permanently out of this world.
          Punchy, yet, dear readers?

Well, there's little reward, not much gain
in accidental homicides
(buses and bombs are so impersonal)
nor angry-fight manslaughter
          or is it - person-slaughters now?
nor careless fatal accidents
like some curious bystander
gets our bullet meant for a cop.

What really tickles a murderer's funny bone
- deserving a wide-eyed grin -
is when the foolproof, months-long
 plan works,   so headlines read
          "No Known Suspects"!

Don't frown at me, judgmental readers.

If murderers aren't humorous,
how come so many cartoon characters
are always trying to knock each other off,
Road Runner or Popeye,
each plan more ridiculous than the last episode?
            Is it plausible that jokes are
            based on mass-avoided truths?

Most of us are too afraid
to even think of murdering:
            our wayward spouse, our annoying child,
            our demanding parents,
that loud-mouthed mayor, THE aggravating agent,
those garbage dumping neighbours

_____

add your own favourite target,
as we've all been warned,
            "to think it is to do it, to be guilty."

Well, some few people - murderers - think the joke is on us,
lily-livered readers of mysteries, only living vicariously
through hundreds of murderous tales
'cause we're too scared   to plan crimes of our own.

Ever wonder, why romances are the most
sold books - crime stories come second -
yet editors keep asking for humour?
Guess more of us crave love than harm, still
maybe many readers need a perfect plan
for their personal, private murder.

What is your weapon of choice:
            razor blades, mustard gas or acid brownies?

_____

Just fill in the blank, if we dare!
Yet all enjoy the horror, the suspense, the power,

even admire the cleverness of devilish plans
become in awe of another's brutal passions,
murderers seeming so focussed, so alive.

Do we, dear readers, hope for justice before the last page,
so we can continue to believe
that crime is NOT worth the punishment?
       Well, if we use someone else's illicit thoughts
       OK - second hand , repeat crimes are not so bad,
but if we live backwards, we are evil.
       What if we face eternity in hell   with our victim(s)?

It's enough to murder our minds,
and then who's laughing?

DANCIN'

Momma's goin' dancin' tonight!

Gonna kick up these old heels
Swing on that shiny pine floor
Stamp feet to that drum beat.

Momma's goin' dancin' tonight!

Gonna grab me a dancin' man
One full of rhythm,
in tight pants, that's my Jim
One full of heat,
in silky shirts, that's my Pete.

Momma's goin' dancin' tonight!

Gonna circle these warm arms
'Round his pulsin' chest
And you, can guess the rest!
Momma's still gotta lotta charms.

Momma's goin' dancin' tonight.

Gonna taste those moist lips
with wine pressin' on mine,
Gonna sway these full hips
So I won't be in 'til sunny nine.

Momma's goin' dancin' tonight.

FLYING

Father Blue jay scans from his lookout post
        high in scrub oak tree,
Mother Blue jay swoops from cedar deck
         shells choice sunflower seeds
         donated by watching cottagers.
She crunches them to paste
         wings back to waiting mouths
         quiets screeching bills in nest.
Then it's Dad's turn to feast,
         check for dangerous intruders:
         swift hawk or sly mink,
before he shares some mushy seeds
         as Mom ascends the I-spy branch.

A few carefree, sun-filled June days
         flutter by as baby Jays flap
about their nest demanding more food:
         each one a Dickensonian "Oliver!"
Mom and Dad muzzled them down
         forcing growing birds to stay home
until the teenagers demanded freedom.
         One by one, they tumble out
flapping and flipping in free fall:
         one by one, they fly or not -
Mom and Dad squawk advice, even love,
         but they can only peer from afar -
         one by one, they fly or not.

FUTTEMANS

As kids we called them 'funny mans'
          or 'funny cookies'
as every quick fried shape
of rolled and knotted
sweet dough bubbled and browned
into its own person.

"Stand back! Grease splatters hurt."
Firm warnings as we dragged
wooden kitchen chairs closer
- our viewing platforms
of fryin' kettle and black McCleary stove.

Each Christmas season/our taste of Sweden,
we waited and whined,
"Today? Can we make funny mans today?"
Of course, Mom did all the making,
we did all the testing and tasting
lip smacking up any broken
crisp bits, those spare limbs
or bodies that were not fit
for company, whole specimens so
neatly arranged on a Yule platter
all perfectly coated with icing sugar.

"Stop! Wait until I can dust them in a bag."
Mom's voice softened with a twinkle
or a tear in her eyes,
as she understood how long a few more
minutes for four or five year olds.

We giggled as kids imagining
some monster "wind-breaker"
 - as 'futte' seemed an obscene body sound -
blowing holes through some original
whole cookies as he 'putt putt' ed
around some celestial kitchen
so that today modern cooks create
finger-holed sweet morsels
in his Futteman's honour.

"Get your hands off that one! It's not broken."
Just when we thought Mom wasn't looking.
Love and magic: main ingredients
of Mom's annual baking bashes,
no uniformly dull, store-bought biscuit shapes -
we sought our 'funny mans', each unique with its own myths
and hoping its future was inside us!

Now three decades and more, after her death,
I still want to share "funny cookie" hours
with Mom.
as no one makes cookies
as fantastic as your Mother.

ACTS OF GOD

Handmade mud banks
shovel by shovel filled
sand bags piled
in miles of borders,
just as useless as lines
of concrete levees,
trying to contain
the massive waters
of the Mississippi in 1993 :
a man-made flood.

Hand cut trees and bushes
fed to cooking fires
for thousands of hungry, cold peoples,
burning woods or denuding lush forests
into barren rocks,
as centuries before,
ash was decreed
needed for man's monuments:
   those man-made pyramids.

Now millions roam these man-made deserts
asking God,
   "Why do my children starve?"

When will some smart lawyer
win a case against insurance
companies for these
   Acts of Man?

"MISSING and PRESUMED"

Unimagined   by grinning
grandfather
at his namesake's
christening
nor by nimble
fingered grandmother
knitting this
lacy blue bootie
that now warms
five rosy toes

is this severed ankle bone
and ragged flesh
weeping blood.

WAR IS A PIMP

WAR is a pimp
who rushes
young bodies
headlong into
disease and death.

WAR is a pimp
who accumulates
pitiless profits
for his politically-
correct owners.

THE YEAR THE PANDAS CAME TO TORONTO

Our summer seasoning was
a little "Chinese in Wasp land",
so Canadians, the eternal spectators,
could continue their
'life as tourists'
while main events continued
to happen elsewhere.

Viewing specimens is so germane
to our own definition   as
not American, nor anti-communist, and
certainly, not mid-East, Central American,
South African, nor even far Asian terrorist!

Actually we live in terror
of ever being extreme,
in anything, about anyone;
we take great pride
in our non-involvement
as if there were an absolute superiority
in pacifist detachment.

We admire the toy-like facade
of the black and white clowns,
(being embraceable ourselves)
these seemingly gentle vegetarians
who so mirror us,
Canadian, an endangered species,
posing stupidly for whatever superpower
wishes to invade our habitat.

YELLOWSTONE PAINT POT

Yellow curls up
a people speaking
wisps to the moon

many moons
drip sour mustard
streak the wall edge

egg odour
signifies a cycle:
beginning/ending

flowing pus
or fragile flowers
as the mind
wills.

YOUNG EYES ASK WHY

Young eyes ask why
as puzzling behind
thick lenses
of gas masks
as they try to see
our reasons,

Even our reason:
which we lost as we swam
neck-deep in
our own sewage
searching for that button
for that last glorious fling
at world destruction.

Don't question, children;
just erase any trace
of humanity,
just corrode and corrupt
all you touch.

Do as we do.

THINKING SHE COULD NOT BE PRETTY

(for Mary)

You can't envy the hollow surface
that size 6 with jutting hip bones
always posed askew, too awkward to cuddle,

those tall, bendable willows
with drug store radiated hair
whose brief days as beauty
never allow one plate of pasta.

Marvel instead at the cheekbones
       of 70 year old Kathryn Hepburn,
       sparkling eyes of Dorothy Livesay
       that sure stance of Pauline McGibbon;

there's beauty in every wrinkle
in the face of Mother Theresa
and a whole world of wonders
in your rich laugh.

QUEEN BITCH MASK

Being a bitch really has its advantages:
           such a name may seem derogatory
but people prejudge your wishes
           standing ready to please
your every whim or whimsy;
           low titles are so useful
when people continually try to remove
           obstacles from you path,
just to avoid one of your tantrums.

Actually, if you play your cards right
           with enough publicity,
you may only have to act
the bitch once - the prima donna role -
           as startling rumours will gossip
round, enlarging, embroidering
your hot and heavy-handedness
           until your very precious passage
           is accompanied by sly looks
           and knowing winks by all
who would soothe your way and theirs
for the sake of supposed peace.

Now if one of that bastard species
with a similar reputation
should block your route,
then purr the playful kitten
to his sleeping dog stance,

for your bitch persona will remain intact,
no matter how many compassionate
or compromising couplings
occur in private.

THOSE WHO LOVED DIANA

Those who loved Diana
were everywhere;
        the Queen of Hearts
was mourned worldwide.

For one tear-jerking week,
the 60's flower children
once again filled the streets
        as millions cried for
        their fairy princess,
briefly believing the old slogan:
        "Make Love - Not War".

Diana, oh moonlit huntress,
you claimed our hearts with one wide, warm smile
        with one blue-eyed glance
        with one athletic stride
or   with one soothing touch.
Oh, Queen of Hearts,
        let not your followers
        be heartless!

Those who loved Diana
for one sorrowing spell,
        aching for that royal mother,
held their children sweetly
hugged each other
even strangers strongly.
        They left their love letters
        and millions of flowers:
a pound of posies in London
a dollar of daisies in Toronto
a pair of petals in Paris,
        flowers for Diana

who they claimed to love dearly,
            flowers to wilt, to dry and be
            "blowing in the wind".

Those who loved Diana
            and there were millions
began visiting old age homes
caring for AIDS victims
and holding hands with lepers.

Those who loved Diana
could not grasp any meaning
in her 'senseless' death.
            Diana, who had so many baubles
but richer still was her inner glow
            that sang
"I've suffered, too.
            I accept some of your pain."
Diana, a survivor of much misery,
            showed us grace
            in a graceless world.

What message then? A Queen of Hearts
            smashed to blood and bone
            in a drunken midnight crash:
just an ordinary tragedy in the dark,
just read your daily, deadly traffic reports.

Diana is gone,
but there are many Rich left
in cities of Europe,
North America and elsewhere;
they glide in glistening limos,
dabbing a tear with white linen
- a public gesture for a fairy princess.

Then these Rich keep demanding

Then these Rich keep demanding
        their pound of flesh:
your brother's leg in Somalia
your sister's arms in Bosnia
your mother's head in Korea.
        They keep demanding their rich,
created by their efficient factories
producing even more efficient land mines:
        O neat, effective personal land mines.

Those who loved Diana:
        do we live by a munitions factory?
        do we own shares in the war machine?
        do we create killing devices?
Where have all the flower children gone?
        Oh, Diana, we need your light.

We all wanted a part
        of that moonlight magic,
        a part of Diana:
some choose the glitter/glamour icon,
others, that shy, lonely schoolgirl image.

We paid for her pictures;
        we made photographers rich
        and sleazy publications thrive.
Now we, hungering millions,
        we, love-starved multitudes
have our separate, silver memory:
        Diana, Queen of Hearts.

How will we honour her?
How will we honour each other?

WINTER ANNEX

Location: Bass Lake, Muskoka, Hwy. 169, Ontario

In the nineteen nineties,
we're imagining those ghost figures
            galloping in galoshes
with billowing-seat long johns
making that dash through foggy
frosty air on icy paths
well-worn by many others
            with nocturnal callings
            to heed one's
            bulging bladder
on a moon-lit January night;
            those Eaton's catalogue
provided daytime reading
            but any time toilet paper.

Now this 'Winter Annex'
set in pine & rock & lake
            - a 'Group of Seven' landscape -
            is a conversation piece,
giving storm proof storage
to excess building lumber
and other cottage repair stuff
needing convenient housing,
so the old outhouse is still
            a convenience.

Now modern septic tanks
replace old lime pit holdings
as cottagers maintain water quality
as well as pampered bums
on indoor heated seats.

APOLOGY TO MY CHILDREN

My impatience is not with you:
too much calls me,
   signals to success or signs of sadness,
   wanted and wanting, I search

while greedy clocks
begrudgingly squeeze out
hurrying hours,
   minutes dash home
   before I can use them.

Myriad opportunities
crook their little fingers,
   hesitating indecisions,
   relentless as ocean waves,
lap through my brain

until each external voice seems
an interruption,
   each outside demand becomes
a plot against
my proper choosing.
Desperately, I scream
   "Leave me alone!"
as one more
   "Mommy, come here!"

and I shall lose my anchor,
flailing in seas of might-have-been
   compass less and
   out of my depth.
Distracted, I may become stuck
in another reality,
   my ever present day-dreams
unable to broadcast myself
on our home channel again.

A PRAYER FOR LOVING JANET

I love Janet.   I pray you can, too.

Before I could love Janet,   or anyone,
I had to learn to love me:
        love this unpredictable,
        joking one minute, crabbing the next,
        unsure me!

If I could change the past,
how many harsh words would I swallow unsaid?
how many foolish acts would I leave undone?

        Yes, I would find patient ears
        for all my children's demands
between too many hours of supply teaching,
night school classes, community committees,
cooking, cleaning, gardening,
- an endless list of excuses -
until there was little or no time
        to hug, to comfort those closest me.

In remembering and in editing,
        we all reach perfection:
given a 2nd or 3rd chance,
        I'd be a perfect me,
but I only live this life once,
        so somehow
I'm to love my stumbling self,
        kicking obstacles out of my way
or   slipping sideways off others,
all those real or imagined enemies.
Me, the supposedly loving mother,
that possessive first love
that displays pride in creations:

"What sweet blond curls!"
or   "What bright blue eyes!":
That selfish pride as if the baby's first steps
or words were mine.

And Janet was an ideal toddler all could love!

But real love comes from brokenness,
            when the bonds break
            and pain separates
so brothers, sisters,
parents drift free,
free to choose other partners, other crutches,
            to learn the love that heals,
            not owns,
            to learn the love that feeds,
            not saps,
to love one's whole self,
            "warts and wealth and all"
thus free to love
            children, brothers, sisters, parents
            again, more, fully, wholly.

            Loving my whole self,
I don't have to degrade everyone
            nor have a need to stab anyone:
accusing, "She said bad words!"   or
            "He did terrible things!"

Stop beating yourself with another's whips
            or useless chains.
Find your own treasure in your hearts;
            Now all I can promise to you
            are houses,
but only you can make them homes
            where love accepts all family,

all friends, without measure or censure.

Think of Janet's creativeness:
        all those wonderful stitches
        her nimble fingers blend,
        all those juicy jams and pies,
            or better still
        all those quick-witted remarks
        cutting clear to the bone.

Janet: a daughter, sister, mother:
        to be loved by herself, for herself,
        her whole, unique self.

I love Janet.   God loves Janet.
Can you love Janet?

HOW MY BLIND STUDENT TAUGHT ME HOW TO SEE!

She trained
        my fingertips to read
        textures and absences,

        my tongue when to spit
        and when to savour,

        my nose when to sniff
        and sneeze and snort,

        my ears to find form in silences
        and fun in sounds
        and more.

Until I had a blind student
        in my poetry workshop,
I did not know how blind
        my eyes were
because I thought that I could see
        so much,
I missed what else my other senses
        could offer me.

Her sightedness enriched our lives
as she felt a natural comfort
        in a darkness we feared;
she counted her steps
        so she knew just where she was
on any black night or bright day,
while we with eyes to see
        were often lost among
strange shapes and foreign streets,

She put colours in her poems
  and conversations,
She knew women would enjoy wearing
  clothes of strawberry or lilac hues
as these have refreshing flavours or scents.

Carefully, she punched and pricked her paper sheet,
somehow mirror-reversing her symbols
so that her fingers could read the paper holes
on the other side: these poems in Braille
  she shared with us.

She let her fingers trace our faces, hair, hands,
  to learn our surfaces,
then in her memory, she joined
  our names and voice patterns
  to our aftershave or perfume,
  our body odour or garlic breath.

She knew us well:
  our insecurities and strengths were clear to her
as she offered suggestions to improve our poems.
She knew both the music
  and the message of words.

She did not believe in black
  being the opposite of the light
that we thought we lived in.
She believed with words   so
  we shared the same universe.
She took us, the world on faith.
  She believed in what she could not see.
People's voices told her more
than oft-fooled, sight-beguiled surfaces told us.

Oh, that more of us could trust
a Heaven we cannot see!

So the blind student taught the teacher ...

hallway mirror reveals

my dead mother peering at me:

puzzled eyes meet

Bibliography

EXCUSES, for all occasions – verse   Highway Book Shop, 1979

SINGING, by Canadian woman prisoners, editor   Highway Book Shop, 1979

YET, WOMAN I AM - poetry Highway Book Shop, 1980

SOMETIMES THE DISTANCE - poetry   Mosaic Press, 1986

THE COLOUR OF WORDS - grammar text   self-published 1990

THE WAITING ROOM - prose   Highway Book Shop, 1993

THINGS UNSAID -poetry Black Moss, 1996

MIX SIX - 6 poets Mekler & Deahl, 1996

UNCIVILIZING - 6 poets   Insomniac Press, 1997

LANGUAGE(S)/PRISON(S) - 4 poets   League of Canadian Poets, 1999

About the Author

Bernice Lever is counting her blessings: 3 children, 3 husbands, 3 living siblings, dozens of cousins and friends, and 2 grandchildren - to date! Her life's adventures are enhanced by dancing angels.

Presently, retiring after 15 years as an English Professor at Seneca College, Toronto, she plans to return to B.C., her birth province. For three decades, she has been active in the Canadian Authors Association, The League of Canadian Poets, and then other writing, editing and teaching associations. In 1998-1999, she was Writer-in-Residence for CAA, Toronto.

For 15 years, she edited the prize-winning literary journal, WAVES, 1972-1987. Bernice has written English textbooks: The Colour of Words, six collections of poetry and published over 200 prose pieces as well as being in numerous anthologies.

Bernice has a 10-year writing, workshopping, and promoting with travelling plan for her first stage of retirement!

Forthcoming:

Seven Stages of Relationships: how-to book & board game

My Cocoon Is Broken – art therapy & healing chants

Lies, for all occasions – a sequel

Two children's picture books and many more poems.

blever a@hotmail.com

Send praise to bfarrar@sympatico.ca and orders to Firefly

www. coleurofwords.com